629.133
Mun

	DATE DUE		

629.133 Munro, Bob
Mun
    Aircraft

AIRCRAFT

Written by Bob Munro
Illustrated by Ian Moores

RSVP

**RAINTREE
STECK-VAUGHN**
P U B L I S H E R S
The Steck-Vaughn Company

Austin, Texas

Editor: Frank Tarsitano
Project Manager: Julie Klaus

Library of Congress Cataloging-in-Publication Data
Munro, Bob.
    Aircraft / written by Bob Munro; illustrated by Ian Moores.
       p.   cm. — (Pointers)
    Includes index.
    Summary: Brief text and labeled illustrations describe different types of aircraft, including long-range airliners, jump jets, supersonic fighter planes, and gliders.
    ISBN 0-8114-6161-0
    1. Airplanes — Juvenile literature. [1. Airplanes.] I. Moores, Ian, Ill.
II. Title.   III. Series.
TL547.M77 1994
629.133—dc20   93-19868
                                     CIP
                                     AC

Printed and bound in the United States

1 2 3 4 5 6 7 8 9 0 VH 99 98 97 96 95 94 93

Foreword

This book is about aircraft which can be seen flying in the skies today. Aircraft are machines which can take off, fly through the air, then land again.

Most aircraft have wings – one on each side – and one or more engines. Commercial aircraft that carry people from one place to another are called airlines. The largest airliners carry hundreds of passengers and have four engines under their wings.

Other types of aircraft are used to fight enemy planes and are called fighters. These are smaller than airliners and usually have only one or two crew members. Fighters usually fly much faster than airliners and fire guns and rockets to shoot down other aircraft.

Aircraft, called gliders, have wings but no engine. They are towed by airplanes into the air and released. Then they are carried along by the flow of air.

There are other aircraft which look very different from airplanes with wings. These are called helicopters. Instead of wings they use long, thin strips of metal, called rotor blades, which turn very fast to help them take off, fly, and land.

Contents

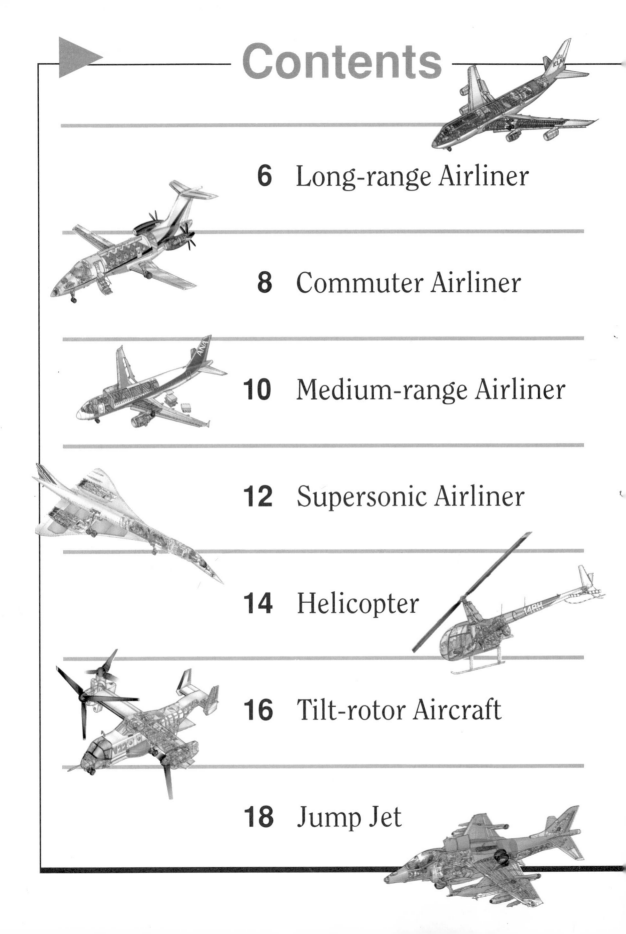

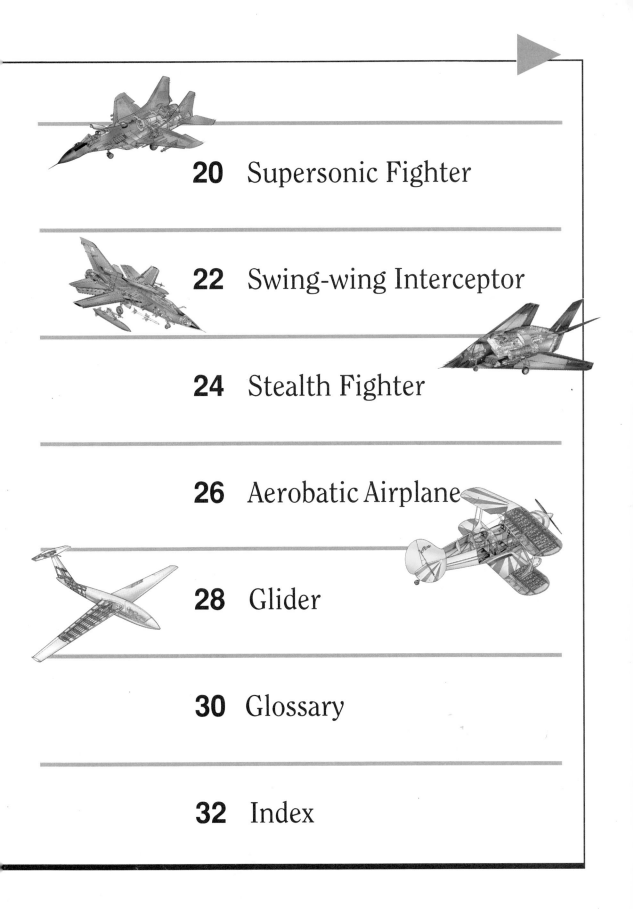

Long-range Airliner

On January 1, 1914 a small flying boat carried one passenger on what was probably the first scheduled flight by an airliner. As air travel became more popular, larger aircraft were needed. In 1969, the biggest modern airliner flew for the first time. This aircraft was the Boeing 747, nicknamed the Jumbo Jet. It is still the biggest airliner flying. It can carry up to 624 passengers and over 57,065 gallons (216,000 l) of fuel, and can fly 6,495 miles (10,475 km) nonstop.

2 The Boeing 747 has a hump-shaped section behind the cockpit. Within this section is a second upper cabin with seats for as many as 69 passengers. A staircase leads down to the main cabin.

3 Large parts of the wing, called flaps, slats, and spoilers, move up and down to help the Boeing 747 land or take off.

Static dischargers

Emergency exit

1 Because it is so big and heavy—nearly 873,000 pounds (395,000 kg) fully loaded—the Boeing 747 needs 16 main landing wheels to take the weight when it is on the ground.

Nosewheel

4 The Boeing 747 is known as a wide-bodied airliner because the main cabin is wide enough for up to 10 seats and two aisles.

5 The Boeing 747 is the longest, widest, and tallest airliner in the world. The tip of the tail fin is about 64 feet (20 m) above the ground.

6 Each wing carries two engines. They are attached to the wings by long metal struts, called pylons.

Aerial

Commuter Airliner

Large, modern airliners can carry hundreds of passengers for thousands of miles to destinations all over the world. But there are also smaller airliners which carry fewer passengers over shorter distances. These are known as commuter airliners. Many of these planes have two engines with propellers. They are fairly inexpensive to operate, so they are popular with many smaller airlines.

The CBA-123 Vector is made in Brazil and Argentina. Its engines are at the back not on or under the wings. This helps reduce noise levels inside the Vector's cabin.

2 There are three seats in the cockpit. The pilot and the copilot sit side-by-side up front. There is a third seat behind them, which is sometimes used by an observer.

1 A radar dish in the nose cone scans the weather many miles ahead of the aircraft. In this way the pilots can avoid any bad weather in front of them.

3 The cabin has seats for 19 passengers in five rows of three and one row of four. Behind the last row of seats is a space used to store the passengers' luggage.

4 The Vector has what is known as a T-tail. It is called this because the vertical tail fin has its tail plane at the top, making it look like a letter *T*.

Air intake

Cargo bay door

5 The engines have six-bladed propellers, which are attached at the back. The engines are called "pusher" engines because their power pushes the Vector forward in the sky.

6 The long, thin wings carry the fuel for the two engines. The fuel is pumped from the wing tanks to both engines through the pipes. The aircraft can fly for 1,150 miles (1,850 km) before refueling.

Navigation light

►Medium-range Airliner

In between the smaller, short-range commuter airliners and the larger, long-range airliners is a group of midsize aircraft that have proved very successful and popular with airlines around the world. These usually have seats for between 120 and 180 passengers. More airliners of this size and capacity have been sold than any other group of airliners.

The Airbus Industrie A320 is one of the most advanced airliners in the world. Five main computers are used to control it when it is flying. Many parts of the aircraft are made of plastic materials, which are lighter but stronger than metal. A320s around the world have flown for a total of over one million hours.

Nose radome

2 The A320's cabin has seats for up to 179 passengers. The front of the cabin has fewer, larger seats. The first-class passengers sit there.

►

The A320 has a very modern cockpit. The pilot and copilot use small levers next to their seats to control the plane and watch the screens in front of them to obtain flight information.

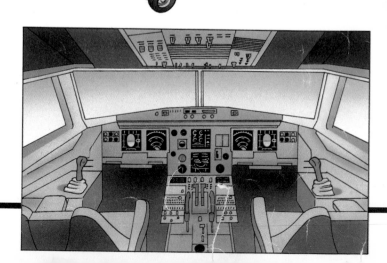

3 Passengers enter and leave the A320 through doors at the front and back of the fuselage. The two doors over the wings are only used to leave the aircraft in an emergency.

4 The end of each wing is shaped like the tip of an arrow. This is called a "winglet". It helps the A320 fly through the air more smoothly.

Cargo pallets

5 Five panels, called spoilers, can be raised to create drag. This helps the A320 slow down and descend for landing.

Slats

1 One engine is carried under each wing. Fuel is pumped to them from the tanks in the wings. The engines are very quiet when the A320 is in flight.

6 Underneath the cabin floor is a space for cargo. Seven large cargo containers can be loaded through a wide door in the fuselage behind the wing.

Supersonic Airliner

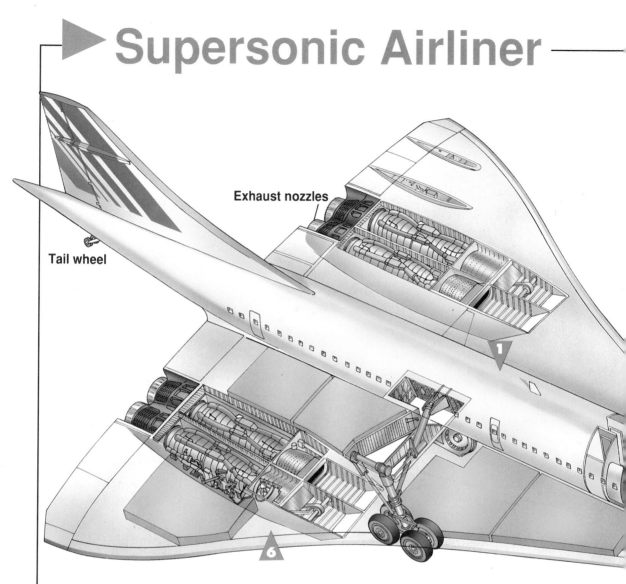

Exhaust nozzles

Tail wheel

1 The fuselage is long and narrow to help the Concorde fly through the air as fast as possible. This is why there are only four seats across the cabin, compared to up to 10 in the Boeing 747.

▶

The Concorde has a very long nose which tapers to a point. This shape helps the aircraft fly smoothly at over 1,300 miles per hour (2,100 kph). Because the length of the nose makes it difficult for the pilot and copilot to see the ground clearly when landing or taking off, it can be lowered to give a better view ahead.

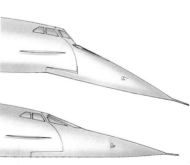

2 Passengers can watch an indicator board which shows the Concorde's speed as it increases to over 1,300 mph (2,100 kph).

3 There are seats for about 100 passengers. Although the windows are small, passengers can see the curvature of the Earth from an altitude of over 59,000 feet (18,000 m).

When the first jet-powered airliners began to enter service during the 1950s, their top speed was less than 600 miles per hour (1,000 kph). This was much faster than the propeller-driven airliners they replaced, but aircraft designers wanted to build even faster planes. Soon, the supersonic airliner, the Concorde, began to take shape. With a top speed of 1,450 miles per hour (2,179 kph)– faster than many jet fighters – it can fly from London to New York in three hours, less than half the time taken by a Boeing 747. It also flies at an altitude of 59,000 feet (over 18,000 m), almost twice the height of a normal airliner.

The Concorde first flew in 1969, but it is still a highly advanced aircraft and the only supersonic airliner in service. British Airways and Air France each have seven Concordes.

4 The Concorde has a flight crew of three. The pilot and copilot sit facing forward, with the flight engineer behind. Another seat can be used by an observer.

6 The Concorde's wing shape is called a delta. This shape helps the Concorde fly smoothly at high speed. Inside each wing are five fuel tanks.

5 On most airliners the nosewheel is under the cockpit, but on the Concorde it is much farther back, underneath the cabin. On takeoff, it swings forward and up.

Weather radar

Helicopter

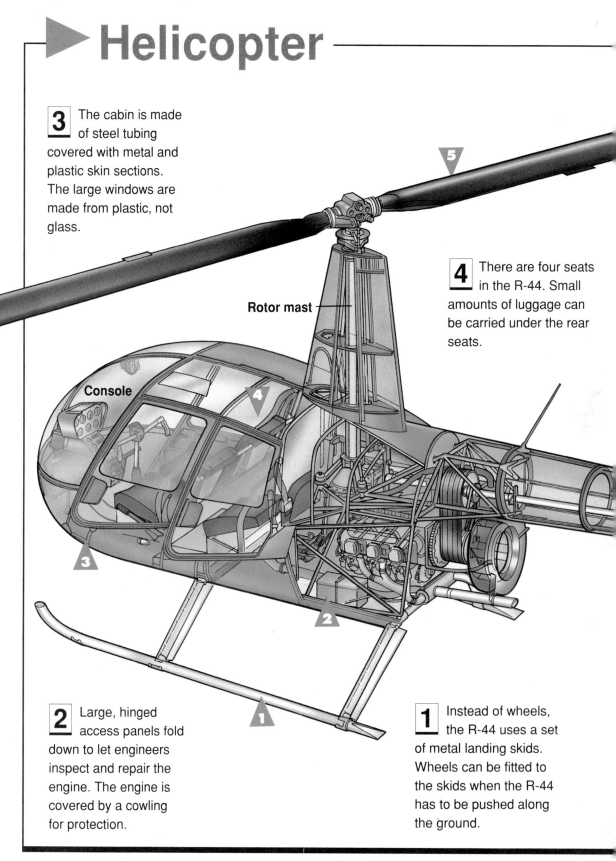

3 The cabin is made of steel tubing covered with metal and plastic skin sections. The large windows are made from plastic, not glass.

4 There are four seats in the R-44. Small amounts of luggage can be carried under the rear seats.

Rotor mast

Console

2 Large, hinged access panels fold down to let engineers inspect and repair the engine. The engine is covered by a cowling for protection.

1 Instead of wheels, the R-44 uses a set of metal landing skids. Wheels can be fitted to the skids when the R-44 has to be pushed along the ground.

5 The two main rotor blades are made of special lightweight metal with stainless steel spars and outer coverings. They are bolted on to the single main rotor mast.

Helicopters have been flying since the 1930s. They are very different from most aircraft because they do not have wings. Instead, they have long, thin blades, called rotor blades, attached above the fuselage as can be seen on the Robinson R-44 shown here. These blades spin very fast to create lift. When there is enough lift, the pilot can tilt the blades forward, backward, or sideways to fly in these directions. The rotor blades turn so fast that they could spin the helicopter around as well, but this is prevented by the small tail rotor which spins in the opposite direction thereby providing balance.

Helicopters can also hover, and can land and take off vertically. This makes them very useful because they do not need runways.

Tail boom

Tail fin

6 A metal rotor guard is fitted around the small tail rotor. This stops the blades from hitting the ground when the helicopter lands.

Tilt-rotor Aircraft

3 The giant propellers, called prop rotors, face forward to enable the Osprey to fly forward like an airplane but tilt upward to enable it to take off, land, and hover like a helicopter.

Rescue hoist

V22

1 On each side of the fuselage is a large bulge called a sponson. This is where the fuel is stored and where the main wheels are housed when the Osprey is flying.

2 Pointing ahead of the nose is a refueling probe.

4 The Osprey's cabin can be used to carry passengers, cargo, or injured people.

5 A wide door near the back of the Osprey can be lowered to form a large ramp. The ramp is used to move troops and cargo in and out of the cabin.

Communications antenna

6 The Osprey's engines are very complicated and need to be checked regularly for any problems. When work has to be done, side panels fold down so engineers can work on the insides.

Access panels

Almost all aircraft with wings are capable only of forward flight. However, some airplanes can also fly up and down and hover like a helicopter. These airplanes are known as tilt-rotors because their engines and propellers can tilt upward like the rotor blades on a helicopter. Because a tilt-rotor aircraft can land and take off vertically, it does not need a long runway, making the airplane much more versatile.

The Bell-Boeing V-22 Osprey is the most famous tilt-rotor aircraft yet built. Its main role is to carry troops and cargo from the decks of ships to bases on land.

►Jump Jet

Most airplanes need long runways to take off and land, so if the runways are damaged, the planes cannot fly. If an air force can destroy an enemy's runways in the early part of a war, the enemy's aircraft will not be able to take part in the war. So runways and airfields are important targets.

Some special aircraft can take off using only a very short runway and can land vertically just like a helicopter. These aircraft are called STOVL (Short Takeoff and Vertical Landing) aircraft, or jump jets. The most successful of these is called the Harrier.

1 The cockpit is covered by a "bubble" canopy. It is called this because it bulges out at the sides and on top and is clear, just like a bubble.

Fuel jettison pipe

◄ When the Harrier's four exhaust nozzles face backward, the Harrier flies forward. When they blast downward, it takes off vertically or hovers.

2 Behind each wing is a small wheel called an outrigger wheel. When the Harrier lands, both of the outriggers act like stabilizers to help it balance.

Tail radome

Air brake

3 On the tail, wings, and fuselage are strips of luminous material. They shine in the dark, so any pilots flying alongside can see just how close they are to the Harrier.

4 The main wheels fold up into the fuselage. They are located behind the nosewheel. This type of arrangement is called a bicycle undercarriage.

6 There are four exhaust nozzles, two on either side of the fuselage, which direct blasts of air and exhaust gases.

5 Underneath each wing are four racks for bombs, missiles, and fuel tanks. Two gun pods, each with 100 shells, are located under the jump jet's fuselage.

Supersonic Fighter

Although large bombers can carry many bombs and missiles, most of them fly quite slowly compared with smaller fighters. The bombers usually do not carry many guns to defend themselves.

Many air forces do not have big bombers. Instead they use smaller aircraft called fighter-bombers. These planes are armed with bombs and air-to-ground missiles for attack, and air-to-air missiles for self-defense.

The MiG-29 is an aircraft designed to shoot down fighter-bombers. The MiG-29 is known as a counter-air fighter, and it relies on super-sonic speed, good maneuverability, and its own missiles to shoot down the fighter-bombers before they reach their targets

1 The pilot wears a special sight built into his helmet. With this, he can aim a missile at a target just by looking at the target through the sight.

2 Most aircraft have one tail fin, but the MiG-29 has two. They are made from carbon fiber, which is lighter than metal but much stronger.

Canopy

When the MiG-29 lands, it is going very fast, so a big parachute is dragged behind it to help it slow down and stop before the plane reaches the end of the runway.

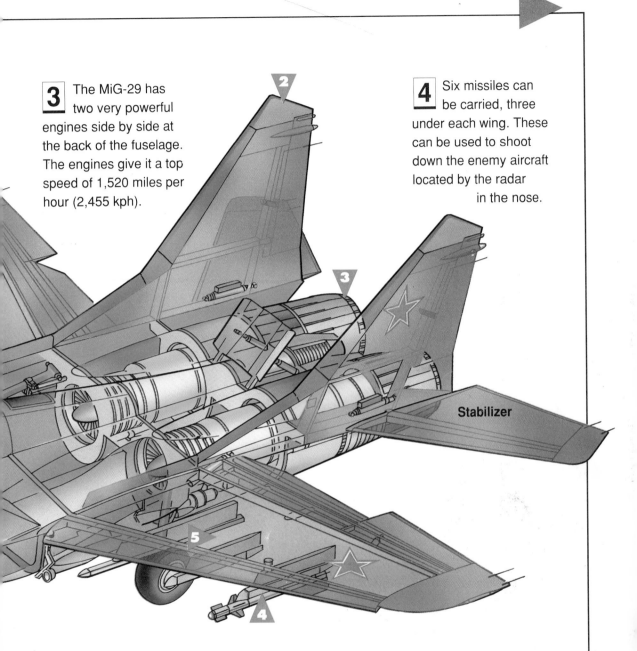

3 The MiG-29 has two very powerful engines side by side at the back of the fuselage. The engines give it a top speed of 1,520 miles per hour (2,455 kph).

4 Six missiles can be carried, three under each wing. These can be used to shoot down the enemy aircraft located by the radar in the nose.

Stabilizer

6 The air intakes for the engines are very close to the ground, so a door closes in each intake when the aircraft is taking off or landing to keep anything from being sucked inside.

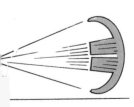

5 The pink areas in the wings show where the fuel tanks are located. Up to 1,150 gallons (4,365 l) of fuel can be carried here, with more in extra tanks under the wings and fuselage.

Swing-wing Interceptor

Almost every air force in the world operates aircraft known as interceptors or fighters. These are often the most important airplanes in an air force. Their role is to take off and find (intercept) enemy aircraft, and stop them from dropping bombs or firing missiles at their targets. Most interceptors have very powerful engines, so they can quickly catch up with enemy airplanes. They are also armed with air-to-air missiles and guns to shoot down any aircraft that do not turn back after interception.

One of the best interceptors is the Panavia Tornado F.3. It has a top speed of 1,670 miles per hour (2,687 kph) and can carry eight missiles and a 27 mm cannon. Tornado interceptors are used by Great Britain and Saudi Arabia.

▼
The Tornado's wings can be moved backward or forward when it is flying. This is known as a variable-sweep wing. An on-board computer chooses the best wing sweep possible, while a large circular pivot moves each wing.

Fuel tank

1 To help the Tornado slow down and stop after landing, the thrust from both of the engines is deflected by metal doors and pushed forward to provide reverse thrust.

2 By moving the wings back, the Tornado becomes much more streamlined. This helps it fly at over twice the speed of sound.

3 The pilot sits in the front cockpit. Behind the pilot is the weapons officer who looks for enemy aircraft on his radar screen. Rocket-powered ejection seats will blast them clear of the aircraft if they need to escape while in flight.

4 The Tornado can be refueled in flight. This is done by the refueling probe sucking in fuel from a feeder line trailing behind a tanker airplane flying in front of the Tornado. The probe is near the pilot where it can be watched closely during refueling.

Slats

6 Four long missiles can be carried underneath the Tornado's belly and four shorter missiles under the wings.

5 The radar is very powerful and can find enemy aircraft flying up to 115 miles (185 km) away from the Tornado.

Stealth Fighter

The shape of most airplanes is designed to be as smooth as possible to help reduce drag and so make the airplane fly faster. But the smooth shape is also very good at reflecting radar signals, so the aircraft can be detected and tracked by radar located on the ground and in the nose of interceptors like the Tornado.

If an airplane can be made invisible to radar, or at least much harder to detect, it is less likely to be intercepted and shot down. To do this, the radar signals have to be absorbed, or dispersed, in different directions. This "stealth," or low-observable technology, is used in the Lockheed F-117A fighter shown here.

4 The V-shaped tail is a very unusual shape for an aircraft. It is also called a butterfly tail because it looks like a pair of butterfly wings.

Windshield

Air data sensor

1 The rectangular grids on either side of the cockpit cover air intakes for the engines. The fine grilles hide the engines from radar waves, so the F-117A remains almost invisible.

2 The F-117A has two weapons bays, each of which can carry one missile or bomb. Extra fuel tanks can be carried in the bays to help increase the F-117A's range.

3 The black skin of the aircraft is actually a spray-on radar absorbent material. This material acts as a sort of cloak, concealing the aircraft by soaking up incoming radar signals.

5 The F-117A's exhaust nozzles are very long and thin. Ceramic tiles absorb most of the hot exhaust gases. This makes it harder for heat-seeking missiles to home in on the aircraft.

6 The F-117A is powered by two engines. They are mounted in the center of the fuselage, with the weapons bays in between. Air for the engines comes through grille intakes.

Main wheel

The F-117A is a very strange looking aircraft. It is made up of many flat, slablike panels. Radar signals hitting them will be deflected in many different directions instead of being reflected straight back.

Aerobatic Airplane

Since World War I, aircraft have been used to carry out amazing twists, turns, loops, and rolls in the air. This is called aerobatics, and specialized aircraft have been built over the years to put on shows that have become more and more spectacular.

Aerobatic aircraft are usually quite small and light, but they have engines that give them enough power to climb and dive quickly. One of the best is the Pitts Special S-2A. The Pitts has two sets of wings, making it a biplane. It weighs just 1,000 pounds (454 kg) when empty and is only 17 feet 9 inches (5.41 m) long and 6 feet 4 1/2 inches (1.94 m) high.

Aileron

1 The inside of each wing is made up of wooden ribs and spars to help reduce weight. These are then covered with fabric panels.

Rudder

Pitts

3

4

2 The two main wheels are almost totally covered by wheel covers, called "pants." These smooth the airflow over the wheels and so reduce drag.

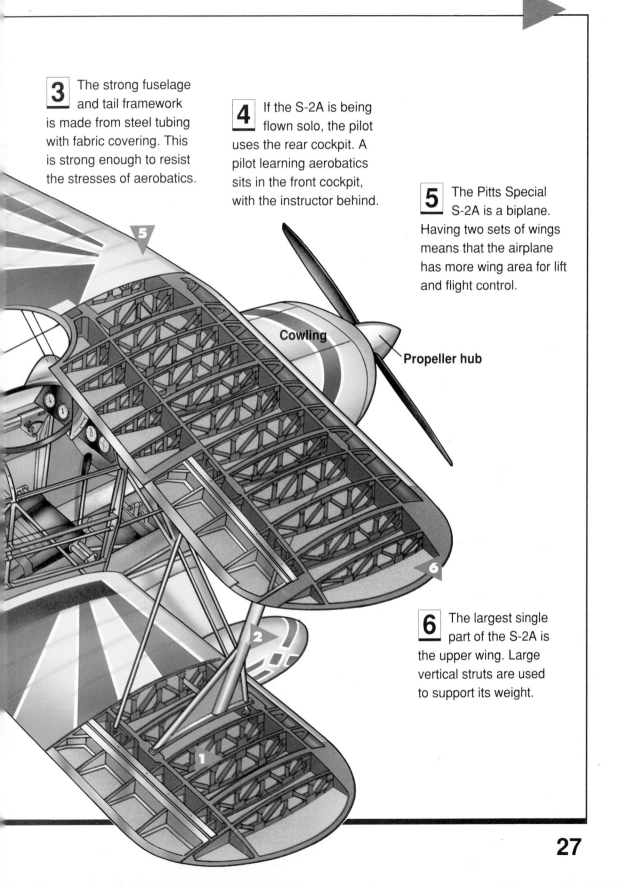

3 The strong fuselage and tail framework is made from steel tubing with fabric covering. This is strong enough to resist the stresses of aerobatics.

4 If the S-2A is being flown solo, the pilot uses the rear cockpit. A pilot learning aerobatics sits in the front cockpit, with the instructor behind.

5 The Pitts Special S-2A is a biplane. Having two sets of wings means that the airplane has more wing area for lift and flight control.

Cowling

Propeller hub

6 The largest single part of the S-2A is the upper wing. Large vertical struts are used to support its weight.

27

Glider

Gliders have wings, a tail plane, and a fuselage just like other aircraft, but they are different because they do not use an engine to help them fly. Instead, gliders are towed into the air by another airplane then use currents of warm air (thermals) which rise up into the sky from the land below to lift them higher. At the top of a thermal, the pilot then glides away, gradually descending and looking for the next thermal to gain more height. A glider can fly for long distances if the pilot is successful at finding and using thermals.

Pitot tube

Fuselage framework

3 Most, but not all gliders, have a "T" tail. The elevators and rudder are moved by sets of wires connected to the pilot's cockpit controls.

2 Gliders are made as light and as strong as possible. Each of the wings has sets of ribs and spars which make a very strong inner frame.

1 All winged aircraft obtain lift by the action of air passing faster over the top of the wing than underneath it. The long, thin wings of a glider are designed to provide maximum lift.

Finding a thermal, the glider rises up and up in a spiral. At the top, the glider soars off, losing height until yet another thermal is found.

4 Small plates in the top of the wings can be raised to create drag. They are called spoilers and help a glider lose speed and height before landing.

6 Gliders have to be light in weight, so many are built of wood with a fabric covering. Some modern designs are made from metal or from fiberglass.

5 Most gliders have a one-person cockpit, but some can hold two. Canopies are usually made of plastic and are often tinted to cut down on the sun's glare.

Glossary

Air data sensor
Probes, such as the pitot, that usually extend ahead of the nose to record information such as air temperature and airspeed

Cabin
The compartment inside an aircraft's fuselage where the passengers are seated

Canopy
The clear, curved covering, usually made from a tough plastic, which covers an aircraft's cockpit(s)

Carbon fiber
Fine strands of carbon used to strengthen composite materials

Cockpit
The compartment where the pilot flies the aircraft. All of the flight controls are located in the cockpit.

Composite
A lightweight but strong material made up of two or more types of fibers, such as fiberglass

Console
The panel in front of the pilot containing the instruments used when flying

Cowling
A removable outer cover used to protect an engine

Drag
Resistance to the motion of an object passing through the air

Elevator
Movable control surfaces, located at the back of each horizontal tail plane. Moving the elevators up makes the aircraft climb; moving them down makes the aircraft descend.

Fiberglass
A strong, yet lightweight, material made from fine strands of glass set in hard plastic

Flap
A movable section at the back of a wing, extended backward to increase the wing's lift on takeoff and downward to increase drag before landing

Fuselage
The body of an aircraft, running from the nose to the tail

Lift
A force created by the airflow passing over an object

Nose radome
The cone-shaped cover used to protect the nose-mounted radar

Pitot tube
See *Air data sensor*

Radar
A radio device or system which sends out short radio waves. The waves are reflected by any object they strike, thereby giving away its position and movement.

Rib
Part of a wing's skeleton. Ribs run from the front to the back of the wing. They form the skeleton with lengthwise spars.

Rotor
The rotating blades above a helicopter which turn at high speed to produce lift

Rudder

The movable section at the back of the tail fin. Moving it to the right makes the aircraft's nose move to the right; moving it to the left makes the nose move to the left.

Runway

A long surface used by aircraft to take off and land

Slats

Sections at the front of a wing which are moved forward to increase lift on takeoff and downward to create drag on landing

Spar

The main part of a wing's skeleton (combining with the ribs) running the length of the wing

Spoiler

Panels in the wing which can be raised up to spoil the flow of air over the wing. They can be used to slow the aircraft down and increase its rate of descent before landing.

Sponson

A short winglike structure projecting from the side of an aircraft. It usually carries the main landing gear and may have extra space for fuel

Stabilizer

See *Tail plane*

Static discharger

Metal strips at the back of the wing that face the rear and are used to discharge static electricity that builds up during a flight

Supersonic

A speed greater than the speed of sound

Swing-wings

An aircraft's wings which can be moved backward and forward in flight

Tail boom

The long, thin boom that joins a helicopter's main cabin with the vertical tail fin unit

Tail fin

The vertical tail at the back of an aircraft. At the back of the tail plane is the rudder.

Tail plane

The horizontal surfaces on either side of the tail fin. At the back of each tail plane is an elevator.

Tail radome

Protective covering for any delicate electronic equipment at the back of an aircraft

Winglet

A small vertical surface on an airliner's wing tip, which improves airflow reducing the amount of fuel used

Index